Amazing Facts About Costa Rica

A collection of amazing facts about Costa Rica

Introduction

Are you ready to embark on an incredible journey to one of the most vibrant and diverse countries on the planet? "100 Amazing Facts About Costa Rica for Smart Kids" is your ultimate guide to discovering the hidden treasures of this amazing land. From lush rainforests and stunning beaches to playful wildlife and rich cultural traditions, Costa Rica is bursting with wonders that will captivate your imagination.

Learn about the cloud forests where quetzals fly, the thrilling jungle adventures, and the heartwarming conservation success stories. Meet the friendly Ticos and Ticas who live by the motto "Pura Vida," embracing life with joy and positivity.

Whether you're a budding explorer or a curious student, this book is packed with fun facts and exciting insights that will make you fall in love with Costa Rica. So grab your explorer's hat, and let's dive into the magical world of Costa Rica, where every page brings a new discovery!

Chapter 1: Geography

- Fact 1: Location and Size

- Fact 2: Climate and Weather

- Fact 3: Mountain Ranges

- Fact 4: Volcanoes

- Fact 5: Rivers and Lakes

Fact 1: Location and Size

Costa Rica is located in Central America, bordered by Nicaragua to the north and Panama to the southeast. It covers about 51,100 square kilometers, making it slightly smaller than West Virginia in the United States. Its diverse geography includes coastal plains, mountains, and valleys. The Pacific Ocean lies to the west, and the Caribbean Sea to the east. This unique positioning contributes to the country's rich biodiversity and varied ecosystems.

Fact 2: Climate and Weather

Costa Rica has a tropical climate with two main seasons: the dry season (December to April) and the rainy season (May to November). The temperature ranges from 21°C to 27°C (70°F to 81°F) but can vary by region. The lush green landscapes during the rainy season attract many visitors. This climate supports diverse ecosystems, from rainforests to dry tropical forests.

Fact 3: The Great Alaska Range

The country is divided by several mountain ranges, including the Cordillera Central and the Cordillera de Talamanca. These ranges contain lush cloud forests and are home to unique wildlife. The mountains are also vital for the country's biodiversity and water sources. They offer numerous hiking trails with stunning views for adventurers.

Fact 4: Volcanoes

Costa Rica has over 60 volcanoes, with six currently active. The Arenal Volcano, known for its perfect cone shape, is a major tourist attraction. Volcanoes play a crucial role in shaping the country's landscape and providing geothermal energy. Visitors can explore trails and enjoy nearby hot springs heated by volcanic activity.

Fact 5: Rivers and Lakes

Costa Rica is rich in rivers, which are vital for irrigation, drinking water, and hydroelectric power. The Río San Juan, which forms part of the border with Nicaragua, is the longest river. The abundance of freshwater resources supports both agriculture and wildlife. Rivers also provide opportunities for activities like white-water rafting and kayaking. Lake Arenal, the largest lake, is popular for windsurfing and fishing, drawing tourists from around the world.

Chapter 2: Biodiversity

- Fact 6: National Parks

- Fact 7: Unique Wildlife

- Fact 8: Bird Species

- Fact 9: Marine Life

- Fact 10: Rainforests

Fact 6: National Parks

Costa Rica boasts over 25% of its land designated as protected national parks and reserves. These parks preserve the country's rich biodiversity and stunning landscapes. Popular parks include Manuel Antonio, Tortuguero, and Corcovado, each offering unique experiences for visitors. They also serve as research hubs for scientists studying tropical ecosystems.

Fact 7: Unique Wildlife

Costa Rica is home to a diverse array of wildlife, including sloths, jaguars, and tapirs. It is one of the most biodiverse countries in the world, hosting around 5% of the planet's species. Many animals can be spotted in their natural habitats, making it a paradise for nature lovers. Conservation efforts aim to protect endangered species and their habitats.

Fact 8: Bird Species

With over 900 species, Costa Rica is a birdwatcher's haven. The resplendent quetzal and scarlet macaw are among the most iconic species. Many bird species are found in the various ecosystems, from coastal mangroves to mountainous cloud forests. Birdwatching tours and festivals celebrate the country's avian diversity.

Fact 9: Marine Life

Costa Rica's waters are teeming with marine life, including dolphins, whales, and sea turtles. Both the Pacific and Caribbean coasts offer excellent opportunities for snorkeling and diving. The coral reefs and underwater ecosystems attract divers from around the world. Marine protected areas ensure the conservation of critical habitats.

Fact 10: Rainforests

Costa Rica's rainforests are rich in biodiversity, housing countless plant and animal species. The lush greenery and dense canopies provide essential habitats for wildlife. Visitors can explore these vibrant ecosystems through guided hikes and canopy tours. Ecotourism initiatives promote sustainable practices to minimize environmental impact.

Chapter 3: History

- Fact 11: Pre-Columbian Era

- Fact 12: Spanish Colonization

- Fact 13: Independence

- Fact 14: Historical Landmarks

- Fact 15: Famous Historical Figures

Fact 11: Pre-Columbian Era

Before the arrival of Christopher Columbus, Costa Rica was inhabited by indigenous peoples such as the Chorotega, Huetar, and Bribri. They lived in small tribes and engaged in agriculture, pottery, and trade. Their cultural artifacts, like stone spheres found in the Diquís Delta, showcase their advanced craftsmanship.

Fact 12: Spanish Colonization

Costa Rica was colonized by the Spanish in the 16th century. The colonization process was relatively peaceful compared to other regions in Latin America, with fewer indigenous populations and less focus on extracting resources like gold and silver. This contributed to a unique cultural blend with Spanish influences and indigenous traditions.

Fact 13: Independence

Costa Rica gained independence from Spain on September 15, 1821, along with other Central American countries. Initially part of the Mexican Empire and later the United Provinces of Central America, it finally became a sovereign nation in 1838 after the dissolution of the federation. This period marked the beginning of Costa Rica's journey towards establishing a stable democratic republic.

Fact 14: Historical Landmarks

Historical landmarks in Costa Rica include the Orosi Church, built in 1743 and one of the oldest churches in the country. The National Theatre of Costa Rica, inaugurated in 1897, is a cultural icon known for its neoclassical architecture and hosting performances and events. These landmarks reflect Costa Rica's architectural and artistic heritage.

Fact 15: Famous Historical Figures

Famous historical figures include Juan Rafael Mora Porras, a national hero known for leading Costa Rica during the National Campaign against William Walker's filibuster and promoting modernization efforts. Other notable figures include Braulio Carrillo Colina, a prominent political figure who served as Head of State and contributed to the country's infrastructure development. Their legacies continue to influence Costa Rican society and politics today.

Chapter 4: Government and Politics

- Fact 16: Democratic System

- Fact 17: No Standing Army

- Fact 18: Famous Presidents

- Fact 19: National Symbols

- Fact 20: Political Stability

Fact 16: Democratic System

Costa Rica operates under a democratic system, with periodic free and fair elections for the presidency and legislature. The country prides itself on its stable democracy and respect for human rights, making it one of the oldest democracies in Latin America. This system includes multiple political parties that participate in elections, ensuring diverse representation.

Fact 17: No Standing Army

Costa Rica abolished its army in 1948, following a brief civil war. Since then, it has remained a peaceful nation and has focused on investing in education, healthcare, and environmental conservation instead of military expenditures. This decision has allowed Costa Rica to allocate resources towards social development and sustainable initiatives.

Fact 18: Famous Presidents

Famous presidents of Costa Rica include José Figueres Ferrer, who abolished the army and promoted social reforms in the mid-20th century. Óscar Arias Sánchez won the Nobel Peace Prize in 1987 for his efforts to promote peace in Central America. These leaders have left lasting legacies and shaped Costa Rican society through their policies and initiatives.

Fact 19: National Symbols

Costa Rica's national symbols include the flag, which consists of five horizontal stripes—blue, white, red, white, and blue—with a coat of arms in the center. The coat of arms features three volcanoes and the Pacific and Caribbean oceans, symbolizing Costa Rica's geographical features and commitment to peace. The national anthem, "Noble patria, tu hermosa bandera," celebrates the country's heritage and unity.

Fact 20: Political Stability

Costa Rica is known for its political stability, with a long history of peaceful transitions of power and low levels of corruption compared to other Latin American countries. This stability has contributed to its reputation as a safe and attractive destination for tourism and investment. The country's strong institutions and commitment to democratic principles underpin its political resilience.

Chapter 5: Culture

- Fact 21: Languages

- Fact 22: Traditional Music

- Fact 23: Dance Forms

- Fact 24: Festivals

- Fact 25: Traditional Clothing

Fact 21: Languages

Spanish is the official language of Costa Rica and is spoken by the vast majority of the population. English is also widely understood, especially in tourist areas and among younger generations. Indigenous languages such as Bribri and Cabécar are spoken by smaller communities, reflecting the country's linguistic diversity. Efforts are underway to preserve and promote indigenous languages through education and cultural initiatives.

Fact 22: Traditional Music

Costa Rican traditional music reflects a mix of influences, including Spanish, African, and indigenous rhythms. The marimba, a wooden xylophone-like instrument, is considered the national instrument and is central to traditional music performances. Other instruments like guitars, drums, and flutes are also commonly used, each contributing to the vibrant musical tapestry of Costa Rica.

Fact 23: Dance Forms

Popular traditional dance forms in Costa Rica include the "punto guanacasteco," originating from the Guanacaste region, characterized by lively footwork and colorful costumes. The "baile de los diablitos" (dance of the little devils) is another significant indigenous dance performed in Boruca, celebrating ancestral traditions and storytelling through dance. These dances are often accompanied by music and rituals that date back centuries.

Fact 24: Festivals

Costa Rica celebrates various festivals throughout the year, blending religious, cultural, and historical themes. The Fiestas de Palmares is one of the largest and most popular festivals, featuring bullfights, rodeos, music, and traditional food. Semana Santa (Holy Week) and Independence Day (September 15th) are also widely celebrated with parades, fireworks, and cultural events, showcasing the country's rich traditions and community spirit.

Fact 25: Traditional Clothing

Traditional clothing in Costa Rica varies by region and cultural heritage. In rural areas, women may wear brightly colored dresses with floral embroidery, while men often dress in white shirts, trousers, and wide-brimmed hats, reflecting agricultural traditions and practicality. Indigenous communities preserve their unique clothing styles, incorporating natural fibers and intricate patterns that signify their identity and connection to the land.

Chapter 6: Economy

- Fact 26: Agriculture

- Fact 27: Coffee Production

- Fact 28: Tourism

- Fact 29: Technology Sector

- Fact 30: Trade Partners

Fact 26: Agriculture

Agriculture plays a significant role in Costa Rica's economy, with key crops including bananas, pineapples, and sugar cane. The fertile lands and diverse climates support a wide range of agricultural activities, contributing to both domestic consumption and export markets. Sustainable farming practices are increasingly emphasized to protect the environment and ensure long-term productivity.

Fact 27: Coffee Production

Costa Rica is renowned for its high-quality coffee production. Arabica beans, grown in the fertile volcanic soils of regions like Tarrazú and Naranjo, are prized for their rich flavor and aroma. Coffee farming is an important part of the country's agricultural heritage and export economy, promoting eco-friendly practices like shade-grown coffee.

Fact 28: Tourism

Tourism is a major driver of Costa Rica's economy, attracting millions of visitors each year. The country's natural beauty, biodiversity, and ecotourism opportunities draw travelers seeking adventure and relaxation. Popular activities include wildlife viewing, surfing, and exploring national parks. Sustainable tourism initiatives aim to preserve Costa Rica's natural wonders for future generations.

Fact 29: Technology Sector

Costa Rica has developed a thriving technology sector, known for its skilled workforce and favorable business environment. The country hosts numerous multinational tech companies that benefit from its educated workforce and stable political climate. Outsourcing services and software development are key components of this sector, driving innovation and economic growth.

Fact 30: Trade Partners

Costa Rica's main trade partners include the United States, China, and the European Union. The United States is the largest export market for Costa Rican goods, particularly agricultural products and medical devices. Trade agreements, such as CAFTA-DR with the US, have boosted Costa Rica's access to international markets, enhancing economic stability and diversification.

Chapter 7: Education

- Fact 31: Literacy Rate

- Fact 32: School System

- Fact 33: Universities

- Fact 34: Educational Achievements

- Fact 35: Student Life

Fact 31: Literacy Rate

Costa Rica boasts a high literacy rate, with over 97% of the population being literate. The government prioritizes education, ensuring access to quality schooling for all citizens. This focus on education has contributed to the country's overall development and social progress. Literacy programs target rural and underserved areas, reducing disparities. The emphasis on education reflects Costa Rica's commitment to human capital and sustainable growth.

Fact 32: School System

The Costa Rican school system includes primary, secondary, and tertiary education. Primary education is mandatory and free, covering six years of schooling. Secondary education is divided into two cycles, and many students continue to university or vocational training. The government provides resources and support to ensure that all children have access to education.

Fact 33: Universities

Costa Rica is home to several reputable universities, including the University of Costa Rica (UCR) and the Costa Rica Institute of Technology (TEC). These institutions offer a wide range of programs and are known for their research and innovation. They play a crucial role in shaping the country's educated workforce. Scholarships and financial aid are available to support students from diverse backgrounds.

Fact 34: Educational Achievements

Costa Rica's commitment to education has led to high rankings in various educational indices. The country emphasizes critical thinking, environmental education, and bilingualism in its curriculum. Students consistently perform well in science and mathematics, reflecting the quality of the educational system. Innovative teaching methods help prepare students for global challenges.

Fact 35: Student Life

Student life in Costa Rica is vibrant, with numerous extracurricular activities, clubs, and cultural events. Universities encourage participation in sports, arts, and community service. This holistic approach to education fosters personal growth and social responsibility among students. Many campuses offer exchange programs that enhance cultural experiences and global perspectives.

Chapter 8: Sports

- Fact 36: Popular Sports

- Fact 37: Famous Athletes

- Fact 38: World Cup Appearances

- Fact 39: National Teams

- Fact 40: Sports Facilities

Fact 36: Popular Sports

Soccer is the most popular sport in Costa Rica, with passionate fans and numerous local clubs. Other popular sports include basketball, volleyball, and surfing, which take advantage of the country's natural landscapes. Surfing competitions attract both local and international athletes to Costa Rica's famous beaches, contributing to its reputation as a surfing destination.

Fact 37: Famous Athletes

Costa Rica has produced several famous athletes, including soccer stars like Keylor Navas, a celebrated goalkeeper who has played for top European clubs. Track and field athlete Nery Brenes has also gained international recognition, winning gold in the 400 meters at the World Indoor Championships. Their achievements inspire young athletes nationwide.

Fact 38: World Cup Appearances

Costa Rica's national soccer team, known as "La Sele," has qualified for the FIFA World Cup multiple times. Their best performance was in 2014 when they reached the quarterfinals, surprising many with their skill and determination. This achievement boosted the nation's pride and enthusiasm for soccer, solidifying its place in international sports.

Fact 39: National Teams

In addition to soccer, Costa Rica has national teams for sports like basketball, volleyball, and rugby. These teams participate in regional and international competitions, showcasing the talent and dedication of Costa Rican athletes. The country supports sports development through various youth programs and initiatives, nurturing future champions.

Fact 40: Sports Facilities

Costa Rica boasts a variety of sports facilities, including stadiums, arenas, and recreational centers. The National Stadium in San José, the largest in the country, hosts major sporting events and concerts. Many communities also have access to local sports complexes that encourage participation in athletics and fitness, promoting a healthy lifestyle among citizens.

Chapter 9: Food and Cuisine

- Fact 41: Traditional Dishes

- Fact 42: Tropical Fruits

- Fact 43: Coffee Culture

- Fact 44: Street Food

- Fact 45: Popular Restaurants

Fact 41: Traditional Dishes

Costa Rican cuisine features traditional dishes like "gallo pinto," a rice and beans dish often served for breakfast, and "casado," a lunch staple combining rice, beans, plantains, salad, and a choice of meat. These dishes reflect the country's agricultural heritage and simple, flavorful cooking style. Seafood dishes are also popular along the coast, highlighting fresh catches from the Pacific and Caribbean.

Fact 42: Tropical Fruits

Costa Rica is abundant in tropical fruits such as pineapple, mango, papaya, and guava. These fruits are enjoyed fresh, juiced, or as ingredients in dishes like fruit salads and desserts. The fertile soils and diverse climates allow for year-round cultivation and availability of a wide variety of fruits. Exotic fruits like starfruit (carambola) and pitahaya (dragon fruit) are also cherished for their unique flavors.

Fact 43: Coffee Culture

Coffee culture is integral to Costa Rican daily life and economy. The country is renowned for producing high-quality Arabica coffee beans, with coffee plantations offering tours to educate visitors about the cultivation and processing of coffee. "Café chorreado," or drip-brewed coffee, is a popular preparation method. Coffee shops (cafeterías) are community hubs where locals gather to socialize and enjoy their favorite brew.

Fact 44: Street Food

Costa Rica offers a variety of delicious street foods, such as "empanadas" (filled pastries), "tamales" (steamed corn dough filled with meats or vegetables), and "chorreadas" (corn pancakes). These affordable and flavorful snacks are often sold by vendors in markets, parks, and street corners throughout the country. Street food vendors often showcase regional specialties, adding to the culinary diversity.

Fact 45: Popular Restaurants

Costa Rica boasts a diverse culinary scene with popular restaurants offering a range of international and traditional dishes. "La Esquina de Buenos Aires" in San José is renowned for its Argentine steaks, while "Soda Tapia" in Heredia serves authentic Costa Rican dishes in a casual setting favored by locals and tourists alike. Fine dining establishments like "Alma de Amón" in San José blend local ingredients with contemporary techniques, appealing to food enthusiasts.

Chapter 10: Environment and Conservation

- Fact 46: Eco-Friendly Policies

- Fact 47: Renewable Energy

- Fact 48: Wildlife Reserves

- Fact 49: Environmental Education

- Fact 50: Conservation Success Stories

Fact 46: Eco-Friendly Policies

Costa Rica is renowned for its eco-friendly policies, including initiatives to protect biodiversity, promote sustainable tourism, and reduce carbon emissions. The government's commitment to conservation has led to the establishment of protected areas and strict regulations to preserve natural resources. These policies have made Costa Rica a global model for environmental stewardship.

Fact 47: Renewable Energy

Costa Rica generates over 99% of its electricity from renewable sources, including hydroelectric, wind, and solar power. This remarkable achievement highlights the country's leadership in clean energy and its commitment to sustainable practices. By investing in green technology and reducing reliance on fossil fuels, Costa Rica serves as a global model for environmental responsibility and innovation.

Fact 48: Wildlife Reserves

Costa Rica is home to numerous wildlife reserves and national parks, such as Corcovado National Park and Tortuguero National Park. These protected areas safeguard diverse ecosystems and endangered species, offering opportunities for ecotourism and scientific research. Conservation efforts within these reserves are crucial for preserving Costa Rica's rich biodiversity.

Fact 49: Environmental Education

Environmental education is a priority in Costa Rica, with programs in schools and communities promoting conservation practices and biodiversity awareness. Hands-on learning experiences in nature foster a deeper appreciation for the environment among children and adults alike. This educational approach ensures future generations are equipped to protect Costa Rica's natural heritage.

Fact 50: Conservation Success Stories

Costa Rica has celebrated conservation success stories, including the recovery of species like the green sea turtle and the scarlet macaw through targeted conservation efforts. Community involvement and sustainable practices have played crucial roles in these achievements, inspiring similar initiatives globally. These successes demonstrate the effectiveness of Costa Rica's conservation strategies and encourage ongoing efforts worldwide.

Chapter 11: Places to Visit

- Fact 51: San José

- Fact 52: Arenal Volcano

- Fact 53: Monteverde Cloud Forest

- Fact 54: Manuel Antonio National Park

- Fact 55: Tortuguero National Park

Fact 51: San José

San José, Costa Rica's capital, is a vibrant city known for its cultural attractions, including the National Theater and Pre-Columbian Gold Museum. It serves as a gateway to the country's natural wonders and offers a blend of historical sites and modern amenities. Visitors can explore bustling markets, dine at diverse restaurants, and experience the lively atmosphere of this urban hub.

Fact 52: Arenal Volcano

Arenal Volcano, with its perfect cone shape, is a prominent feature of Costa Rica's landscape. Visitors can enjoy activities such as hiking, hot springs, and wildlife viewing in the surrounding Arenal Volcano National Park. The area is also known for its geothermal activity, providing opportunities for relaxation in natural hot springs.

Fact 53: Monteverde Cloud Forest

Monteverde Cloud Forest Reserve is renowned for its biodiversity and mystical cloud-covered landscapes. It offers opportunities for birdwatching, hiking on suspended bridges, and experiencing the unique flora and fauna of Costa Rica's cloud forests. The reserve is a haven for nature enthusiasts seeking immersive eco-adventures.

Fact 54: Manuel Antonio National Park

Manuel Antonio National Park, on Costa Rica's Pacific coast, is famous for its beautiful beaches, dense rainforests, and diverse wildlife. Visitors can hike through the park's trails, relax on pristine beaches, and spot animals such as monkeys, sloths, and colorful birds. The park's scenic viewpoints offer stunning vistas of the Pacific Ocean and surrounding coastline.

Fact 55: Tortuguero National Park

Tortuguero National Park, located on the Caribbean coast, is a protected area known for its rich biodiversity and nesting sea turtles. Accessible only by boat or small plane, the park's network of canals and waterways allows visitors to explore its lush rainforests and observe wildlife such as jaguars, manatees, and various bird species. Guided tours offer insights into the park's conservation efforts and unique ecosystems.

Chapter 12: Famous Cities

- Fact 56: San José

- Fact 57: Liberia

- Fact 58: Alajuela

- Fact 59: Heredia

- Fact 60: Cartago

Fact 56: San José

San José is the capital and largest city of Costa Rica, known for its cultural attractions, vibrant nightlife, and historical landmarks like the National Theater and Gold Museum. It serves as the country's political, economic, and cultural center. The city's bustling markets, eclectic cuisine, and lively festivals reflect its dynamic urban character.

Fact 57: Liberia

Liberia is the capital city of Guanacaste Province, known as the gateway to Costa Rica's northwest Pacific region. It offers easy access to popular beaches like Playa del Coco and serves as a hub for eco-tourism and adventure activities. Liberia's lively street markets and traditional cuisine provide a taste of Guanacaste's rich cultural heritage.

Fact 58: Alajuela

Alajuela is Costa Rica's second-largest city and is located in the fertile Central Valley. It is known for its coffee plantations, traditional festivals like the Fiesta de los Diablitos, and its proximity to Juan Santamaría International Airport. The city's welcoming atmosphere and historic charm make it a popular stop for travelers exploring the agricultural heartland of Costa Rica.

Fact 59: Heredia

Heredia, nicknamed the "City of Flowers," is known for its colonial architecture, coffee plantations, and educational institutions like the National University. It offers a tranquil atmosphere and serves as a gateway to the Braulio Carrillo National Park. Heredia's botanical gardens and vibrant cultural scene attract nature enthusiasts and academics alike.

Fact 60: Cartago

Cartago was the capital of Costa Rica until 1823 and is known for its historical significance, including the Basilica of Our Lady of the Angels (Basilica de Nuestra Señora de los Ángeles). It is located in the Central Valley and holds cultural and religious importance for Costa Ricans. Cartago's picturesque surroundings and archaeological sites provide glimpses into the region's ancient civilizations.

Chapter 13: Travel Tips

- Fact 61: Best Time to Visit

- Fact 62: Safety Tips

- Fact 63: Transportation Options

- Fact 64: Health Precautions

- Fact 65: Packing Essentials

Fact 61: Best Time to Visit

The best time to visit Costa Rica is during the dry season, from December to April, when the weather is generally sunny and dry, ideal for outdoor activities and exploring national parks. The peak tourist season falls during these months, so it's recommended to book accommodations and tours in advance. The shoulder seasons of May to November offer lush green landscapes and fewer crowds, though there may be more rain.

Fact 62: Safety Tips

Costa Rica is relatively safe for travelers, but it's advisable to exercise caution, especially in urban areas, and avoid displaying valuables. Always use reputable transportation and accommodations, and stay informed about local conditions. Petty theft can occur in tourist areas, so keeping belongings secure and being aware of surroundings is recommended. Travelers should also carry a copy of their passport and have emergency contact information readily available.

Fact 63: Transportation Options

Transportation options in Costa Rica include rental cars, public buses, shuttles, and domestic flights. Rental cars offer flexibility for exploring remote areas, while buses are a budget-friendly option for traveling between cities and towns. Private shuttles and taxis are convenient for door-to-door transfers, especially for reaching destinations not served by public transportation. Domestic flights are available for longer distances, such as between San José and popular tourist regions like Guanacaste.

Fact 64: Health Precautions

Travelers to Costa Rica should take standard health precautions, including staying hydrated, using insect repellent to prevent mosquito bites (especially in areas with risk of Zika virus), and ensuring vaccinations are up to date based on personal health and travel plans. Medical care is generally good in urban areas, but travelers should have travel insurance that covers medical expenses and emergency evacuation.

Fact 65: Packing Essentials

Essential items to pack for a trip to Costa Rica include lightweight clothing for warm weather, comfortable walking shoes or sandals, a reusable water bottle, sunscreen, insect repellent, and a travel guide or map for navigating the country's diverse landscapes. Additional useful items include a waterproof backpack or daypack for excursions, a hat and sunglasses for sun protection, and a camera or binoculars for wildlife observation.

Chapter 14: Music and Arts

- Fact 66: Popular Bands

- Fact 67: Art Galleries
-
- Fact 68: Famous Artists

- Fact 69: Traditional Crafts

- Fact 70: Music Festivals

Fact 66: Popular Bands

Costa Rica boasts a vibrant music scene with popular bands spanning various genres such as rock, reggae, salsa, and traditional folk. Notable bands include Malpaís, Gandhi, Sonámbulo Psicotropical, and Editus, each contributing uniquely to the country's musical diversity and cultural identity. These bands often blend traditional Costa Rican rhythms with contemporary influences, appealing to both local audiences and international listeners.

Fact 67: Art Galleries

Costa Rica features numerous art galleries that showcase both local and international artists. In San José, the capital city, notable galleries include the Museum of Costa Rican Art, Galería Nacional, and Museo de Arte y Diseño Contemporáneo (MADC). These venues exhibit a wide range of artistic expressions, from traditional to avant-garde, fostering cultural appreciation and creativity. They serve as hubs for artists to showcase their works and for art enthusiasts to explore Costa Rica's rich artistic heritage.

Fact 68: Famous Artists

Costa Rica has produced influential artists who have left enduring impacts on the global art scene. Francisco Amighetti, known for his expressive paintings and prints depicting Costa Rican life, and Ibo Bonilla, celebrated for his abstract and surrealistic artworks, are among the country's most revered artists. Their works continue to inspire and reflect Costa Rica's cultural richness. Their contributions to art have shaped Costa Rican identity and influenced artistic movements beyond the country's borders.

Fact 69: Traditional Crafts

Traditional crafts in Costa Rica encompass a rich heritage of artisanal skills passed down through generations. These include intricately painted oxcarts (carretas), handmade pottery, finely woven textiles like the traditional "tipico" clothing, and delicate wood carvings. These crafts not only showcase the country's artistic talent but also preserve cultural traditions and support local economies. Artisans often use sustainable practices, ensuring these crafts continue to thrive in harmony with Costa Rica's natural environment.

Fact 70: Music Festivals

Costa Rica hosts a variety of music festivals that celebrate diverse genres and cultural influences. The Envision Festival in Uvita is renowned for its fusion of music, art, yoga, and sustainability, attracting a global audience. These festivals not only entertain but also educate audiences about Costa Rican culture and promote environmental consciousness through creative expression.

Chapter 15: Language and Communication

- Fact 71: Spanish Language

- Fact 72: Common Phrases

- Fact 73: Indigenous Languages

- Fact 74: Language Schools

- Fact 75: Media and Communication

Fact 71: Spanish Language

Spanish is the official language of Costa Rica and is widely spoken across the country. It plays a crucial role in daily life, government, education, and business. Costa Rican Spanish has distinct regional variations and is characterized by its clear pronunciation and friendly expressions. Language learning is integral to cultural integration, with many visitors and expatriates enrolling in language courses to enhance their communication skills and understanding of local customs.

Fact 72: Common Phrases

Costa Ricans commonly use phrases like "pura vida" (pure life), which symbolizes a positive outlook and relaxed lifestyle. Other common expressions include "mae" (dude or buddy) and "tuanis" (cool or great), reflecting the country's informal and friendly communication style. These phrases often convey a sense of camaraderie and hospitality, making interactions with locals enjoyable and enriching for visitors.

Fact 73: Indigenous Languages

Costa Rica is home to several indigenous languages, including Bribri, Cabécar, and Boruca, spoken by indigenous communities primarily in remote regions. Efforts are underway to preserve and promote these languages as part of the country's cultural heritage. Language revitalization initiatives involve collaboration with indigenous communities to document oral traditions, teach languages in schools, and celebrate cultural events that highlight linguistic diversity.

Fact 74: Language Schools

Costa Rica offers language schools and immersion programs for international students seeking to learn Spanish. Popular destinations for language learning include San José, Heredia, and Monteverde, where students can immerse themselves in the language and culture. Language schools often incorporate cultural activities such as cooking classes, dance lessons, and excursions to historical sites, providing a comprehensive learning experience beyond the classroom.

Fact 75: Media and Communication

Costa Rica has a diverse media landscape, including newspapers, radio stations, television channels, and online platforms. Major newspapers such as La Nación and Diario Extra provide news coverage on national and international issues. The country also has a vibrant community radio sector that serves local communities with news, music, and cultural programming, bolstered by digital media platforms and social media in shaping public discourse and disseminating information.

Chapter 16: Wildlife

- Fact 76: Endemic Species

- Fact 77: Exotic Birds

- Fact 78: Marine Mammals

- Fact 79: Insects and Arachnids

- Fact 80: Reptiles and Amphibians

Fact 76: Endemic Species

Costa Rica is home to a remarkable array of endemic species, found nowhere else in the world. These include the iconic resplendent quetzal, the colorful golden toad (now possibly extinct), and numerous unique plants and insects. The country's biodiversity hotspots, such as Monteverde Cloud Forest and Corcovado National Park, harbor many of these rare species, contributing to Costa Rica's reputation as a global conservation priority.

Fact 77: Exotic Birds

Costa Rica boasts over 850 bird species, making it a paradise for birdwatchers. Exotic birds like the scarlet macaw, toucans, and hummingbirds dazzle with their vibrant plumage and diverse behaviors. Birdwatching tours are popular, offering enthusiasts opportunities to spot these colorful creatures in their natural habitats and contribute to citizen science efforts.

Fact 78: Marine Mammals

Costa Rica's coastal waters teem with marine life, including various marine mammals such as dolphins, whales, and manatees. The waters off the Osa Peninsula and Golfo Dulce are particularly rich in marine biodiversity, providing crucial habitats for these fascinating creatures and supporting eco-tourism initiatives focused on marine conservation.

Fact 79: Insects and Arachnids

Costa Rica is home to a staggering diversity of insects and arachnids, from iridescent butterflies to venomous spiders. The country's rainforests and cloud forests host an abundance of these small but ecologically significant creatures, contributing to Costa Rica's status as one of the most biodiverse regions on Earth.

Fact 80: Reptiles and Amphibians

Costa Rica harbors a rich diversity of reptiles and amphibians, with over 200 species. Iconic species include the green iguana, poison dart frogs, and the American crocodile. The country's diverse habitats, from tropical rainforests to mangrove swamps, support a wide range of these fascinating creatures, highlighting Costa Rica's role in amphibian and reptile conservation efforts globally.

Chapter 17: Science and Innovation

- Fact 81: Research Institutes

- Fact 82: Scientific Discoveries

- Fact 83: Medical Advancements

- Fact 84: Environmental Research

- Fact 85: Technological Startups

Fact 81: Research Institutes

Costa Rica hosts several research institutes dedicated to various fields such as biodiversity, tropical agriculture, and sustainable development. Institutions like the Tropical Agricultural Research and Higher Education Center (CATIE) and the Tropical Science Center (CCT) play pivotal roles in advancing scientific knowledge and promoting environmental conservation.

Fact 82: Scientific Discoveries

Costa Rica has been the site of significant scientific discoveries, particularly in biodiversity and tropical ecology. Discoveries include new species of plants and animals, insights into tropical diseases, and pioneering research in sustainable agriculture practices. These discoveries contribute to global scientific understanding and conservation efforts.

Fact 83: Medical Advancements

Costa Rica has made strides in medical research and healthcare, with advancements in areas such as tropical medicine, public health initiatives, and healthcare accessibility. Institutions like the Costa Rican Institute for Research and Teaching in Nutrition and Health (INCIENSA) lead research efforts that benefit both local populations and contribute to global health initiatives.

Fact 84: Environmental Research

Environmental research in Costa Rica focuses on biodiversity conservation, climate change mitigation, and sustainable development practices. Organizations like the Costa Rican Amphibian Research Center (CRARC) and the National Biodiversity Institute (INBio) conduct vital research to preserve Costa Rica's natural resources and promote environmental stewardship.

Fact 85: Technological Startups

Costa Rica has a growing ecosystem of technological startups, particularly in sectors such as information technology, biotechnology, and renewable energy. Startup incubators and accelerators like ParqueTec and the Technology Park of Costa Rica (PCTCR) support innovation and entrepreneurship, fostering a culture of technological advancement and economic growth.

Chapter 18: Social Aspects

- Fact 86: Family Life

- Fact 87: Gender Equality

- Fact 88: Social Programs

- Fact 89: Community Festivals

- Fact 90: Public Holidays

Fact 86: Family Life

Costa Rica places a strong emphasis on family life, with close-knit family units playing a central role in society. Extended families often live near each other, providing support and fostering strong social bonds across generations. Family gatherings are important occasions for sharing meals, celebrations, and maintaining traditions, reinforcing the country's cultural values of unity and solidarity.

Fact 87: Gender Equality

Costa Rica has made significant strides in promoting gender equality. Women play active roles in politics, education, and the workforce, with initiatives to reduce gender disparities in wages and leadership positions. The country ranks high in global gender equality indices, reflecting ongoing efforts to empower women through education and economic opportunities.

Fact 88: Social Programs

Costa Rica has implemented various social programs to support vulnerable populations, including healthcare, education, and social assistance programs. The Universal Healthcare System (CCSS) ensures access to healthcare services for all citizens, while social assistance programs provide financial support to low-income families and senior citizens, promoting social inclusion and reducing inequality.

Fact 89: Community Festivals

Community festivals are vibrant celebrations of Costa Rican culture and heritage, featuring music, dance, food, and traditional crafts. Festivals like the Palmares Festival and the Fiestas de Zapote bring communities together to celebrate religious holidays, historical events, and local traditions, fostering community pride and cultural preservation.

Fact 90: Public Holidays

Costa Rica observes several public holidays throughout the year, including religious holidays like Easter and Christmas, as well as national celebrations such as Independence Day and Guanacaste Day. These holidays are marked by parades, fireworks, traditional dances, and cultural events that highlight Costa Rican identity and history, uniting the nation in shared heritage and patriotism.

Chapter 19: Fun Facts

- Fact 91: Quirky Laws

- Fact 92: Interesting Traditions

- Fact 93: Unique Buildings

- Fact 94: Celebrity Visits

- Fact 95: Unusual Sports

Fact 91: Quirky Laws

Costa Rica has some quirky laws, such as a prohibition on building structures within 50 meters of high tide marks to protect coastal ecosystems. Additionally, it's mandatory for public buildings to have a water source for firefighters, reflecting the country's emphasis on safety and environmental conservation.

Fact 92: Interesting Traditions

One interesting tradition in Costa Rica is the "Tope Nacional," a national horse parade held annually in San José to celebrate the country's agricultural heritage. This colorful event features riders showcasing their horsemanship skills and traditional attire, attracting participants and spectators from across the country.

Fact 93: Unique Buildings

The National Theatre of Costa Rica, located in San José, is a stunning example of neoclassical architecture. Built in 1897, it stands as a cultural landmark hosting performances that celebrate Costa Rican artistic talents, including opera, ballet, and concerts by renowned national and international artists.

Fact 94: Celebrity Visits

Costa Rica has attracted numerous celebrities, including Leonardo DiCaprio and Gisele Bündchen, drawn by its eco-tourism attractions and luxurious resorts. Their visits have not only boosted tourism but also highlighted the country's commitment to sustainability and natural conservation efforts.

Fact 95: Unusual Sports

Costa Rica hosts unique sports events like ox-cart racing, a tradition rooted in the country's agricultural history. Teams compete using traditional ox carts adorned with vibrant colors and designs, racing through dirt tracks to showcase rural traditions and skills in a festive atmosphere that celebrates community spirit.

Chapter 20: Future Prospects

- Fact 96: Technological Advancements

- Fact 97: Sustainable Development

- Fact 98: Educational Reforms

- Fact 99: Economic Growth

- Fact 100: Costa Rica's Role in the Global Community

Fact 96: Technological Advancements

Costa Rica is increasingly investing in technological advancements, particularly in renewable energy, biotechnology, and information technology sectors. These innovations aim to enhance efficiency, sustainability, and competitiveness in the global market, positioning Costa Rica as a hub for innovation in Latin America.

Fact 97: Sustainable Development

Costa Rica continues to prioritize sustainable development practices, including conservation efforts, eco-tourism initiatives, and renewable energy projects. These efforts aim to preserve natural resources, mitigate climate change impacts, and promote a green economy that balances economic growth with environmental stewardship.

Fact 98: Educational Reforms

Costa Rica is implementing educational reforms to enhance curriculum standards, teacher training programs, and technological integration in schools. These reforms aim to foster critical thinking, innovation, and global citizenship among students, equipping them with skills necessary for the 21st-century workforce and leadership roles.

Fact 99: Economic Growth

Costa Rica's economy shows steady growth, driven by diverse sectors such as tourism, agriculture, and manufacturing. Efforts to attract foreign investment, improve infrastructure, and support small businesses contribute to sustained economic expansion, creating opportunities for employment and prosperity across the country.

Fact 100: Costa Rica's Role in the Global Community

Costa Rica plays a proactive role in the global community through diplomatic initiatives, environmental leadership, and participation in international organizations. Known for its peace-oriented foreign policy, the country advocates for human rights, environmental protection, and sustainable development on the global stage, influencing global policies and fostering international cooperation.

Conclusion

Congratulations on exploring "100 Amazing Facts About Costa Rica for Young Readers"! You've embarked on a journey through Costa Rica's lush rainforests, vibrant cities, and stunning coastlines. From discovering rare wildlife like sloths and toucans to learning about sustainable living and cultural traditions, Costa Rica has captivated us with its beauty and diversity.

We hope this book has ignited your passion for nature, conservation, and exploration. Remember, Costa Rica's commitment to protecting its natural treasures serves as an inspiration to us all. As you continue to explore the world, carry with you the spirit of pura vida—the pure life—that Costa Ricans cherish.

Thank you for joining us on this adventure through Costa Rica. May your curiosity and love for our planet continue to grow with every new discovery. ¡Pura vida y hasta pronto!

Made in the USA
Monee, IL
04 December 2024

72027603R00069